More Advance Praise for *Flowers as Mind Control* by Laura Minor

Welcome to the unforgettable world of Laura Minor, dear readers. Why is it hard to forget, you might wonder? Because the voices here are unique. "I want to break my yolk," one voice says, "ooze in public spaces / caught in honey while the wheels of old dogs / slog through the dry bread of each day." In this lyrical landscape, you will meet many wonders. You will, for example, meet a neighbor with "dogs around her like fluttering, dirty muses," and a character who announces herself to be a "Lungfish," going about "smoothing my gills into hips, / pulling out the white tide of one life, / breaking open the bubbled heart of another." This world is hard to forget, I am telling you. But why, why is it so? Perhaps because Laura Minor's imagination, as different from ours as it is, captures something of our own: "put my ear to the highest window / to see if it compares to you." Indeed. This book is a terrific debut.

—Ilya Kaminsky, *Deaf Republic*

"I want the muse that will drive me into the ground, / blazing up the wet dirt of my own grave," declares the speaker of Laura Minor's virtuosic debut poetry collection *Flowers as Mind Control.* Whether perambulating city streets, darting through visceral flashes of memory, or paying tribute to inspirations, Minor dazzles with wit and insight. These poems welcome the reader into story fragments that feel all the more gorgeous by their splintering. For example, in "Bildungsroman in Red," "We glow / like twin redheads, whole countries leave / their daughters to careless cowboys / and here— / I am tender as a mouth." Every poem in this book might be your new fight song. Prepare to turn the volume all the way up.

—Mary Biddinger, *Partial Genius*

FLOWERS AS MIND CONTROL

Winners of the John Ciardi Prize for Poetry

The Resurrection Machine by Steve Gehrke,
                    selected by Miller Williams

Kentucky Swami by Tim Skeen, selected by Michael Burns

Escape Artist by Terry Blackhawk, selected by Molly Peacock

Fence Line by Curtis Bauer, selected by Christopher Buckley

The Portable Famine by Rane Arroyo, selected by Robin Becker

Wayne's College of Beauty by David Swanger,
                    selected by Colleen J. McElroy

Airs & Voices by Paula Bonnell, selected by Mark Jarman

Black Tupelo Country by Doug Ramspeck,
                    selected by Leslie Adrienne Miller

Tongue of War by Tony Barnstone, selected by B. H. Fairchild

Mapmaking by Megan Harlan, selected by Sidney Wade

Secret Wounds by Richard Berlin, selected by Gary Young

Axis Mundi by Karen Holmberg, selected by Lorna Dee Cervantes

Beauty Mark by Suzanne Cleary, selected by Kevin Prufer

Border States by Jane Hoogestraat, selected by Luis J. Rodríguez

One Blackbird at a Time by Wendy Barker,
                    selected by Alice Friman

The Red Hijab by Bonnie Bolling, selected by H. L. Hix

All That Held Us by Henrietta Goodman, selected by Kate Daniels

Sweet Herbaceous Miracle by Berwyn Moore,
                    selected by Enid Shomer

Latter Days of Eve by Beverly Burch,
                    selected by Patricia Spears Jones

Dark Braid by Dara Yen Elerath, selected by Doug Ramspeck

Flowers as Mind Control by Laura Minor, selected by John Hodgen

FLOWERS AS MIND CONTROL

Poems

Laura Minor

Winner of the John Ciardi Prize for Poetry
Selected by John Hodgen

BkMk Press
University of Missouri-Kansas City

BkMk Press
bkmkpress.org

Executive Editor: Christie Hodgen
Managing Editor: Ben Furnish
Assistant Managing Editor: Cynthia Beard
Intern: Aidan Powers

BkMk Press and the John Ciardi Prize for Poetry wish to thank Walter Bargen, Susan Cobin, Greg Field, Henrietta Goodman, Lindsey Martin-Bowen, Linda Rodriguez, Maryfrances Wagner.

Missouri
Arts Council
The State of the Arts

Financial assistance for this project was provided by the Missouri Arts Council, a state agency.

For a complete list of donors, see page 72.

Library of Congress Cataloging-in-Publication Data

Names: Minor, Laura, author.
Title: Flowers as mind control : poems / by Laura Minor.
Description: Kansas City, MO : BkMk Press, University of Missouri-Kansas City, 2021. | Summary: "These poems, which range across rural Florida and Georgia as well as Los Angeles and New York City, include considerations of homesickness, memory, music, alcohol, love, and loss. Winner of the John Ciardi Prize for Poetry, selected by John Hodgen"-- Provided by publisher.
Identifiers: LCCN 2021012879 | ISBN 9781943491308 (paperback)
Subjects: LCGFT: Poetry.
Classification: LCC PS3613.I6573 F58 2021 | DDC 811/.6--dc23
LC record available at https://lccn.loc.gov/2021012879

ISBN: 978-1-943491-30-8

This book is dedicated to women everywhere
who refuse to give up their dreams

Contents

Never forget:
we walk on hell,
gazing at flowers.

— Kobayashi Issa

Foreword

If you're looking for a voice that's fiercely fresh and new, one that embodies the deepest and best poetry ethic, writing because one desperately has to and would die without doing, then consider Laura Minor in her new *Flowers as Mind Control*. Here is a true original, one who can both conceive and convey a poem titled "The Ricketiest Song in the World," in which she watches, like some wild new Whitman, "lightning cook the weeds around my feet," saying her own want, that she is ready "to dive into bricks / looking for you." Who wouldn't want to hear more of that voice, or be the recipient of that haunted devotion? Minor makes clear her sense of her role, saying, in the same poem:

> I am a cavernous, traveling siren
> screaming slow-jams, and yet, I'm not yet done
> feeding the south with ballads
> that butter the sad mouths of strangers.

Minor is not just a gifted wanderer. She's done her work, knowing and pledging allegiance to Ovid's want, his wisdom about exile and loss, saying, "I want to be with you / any way I can." She also imagines the work of the conveyor belt and the loading dock at the seed factory. She is old enough to know that nature, "cruel in its blazing craft," will turn her arms to dust, but she is vibrant and young enough to say, "I will turn myself into rain." She can praise the iconic Aqua Queen, Esther Williams, stepping out of a clam shell, angelic, "pouring herself from the bubbling pinhead of a Hollywood geyser into the depths," and yet also can ask, seeing a dead deer in the back of a truck bed, "Can we sing for the buck stiffening in the chill?"

Minor's is that life, both young and old, which some could look to emulate, and some could look back to see where they went wrong. She is a freestyle teacher, learning by doing, with that fierceness again, of perceiving, of knowing that solitude can be a largesse, and that living, that "falling forward in years," are necessary juxtapositions providing that tension from which the best poetry rises. She states, almost proudly, that "people and their oval faces, like creamy footprints of beaches, are her "King and [her] Kung Fu." Here is a poet, many-voiced, who at any cost is gathering groats of wisdom. Try these for size, this from "I Don't Camp Well,"

> Coupling and terror are just two trees
> in the same shallow water, roots comingled

with the sea level's dooming groan, and me,
the lone, winsome variable of nature.

And, this from "Recidivism,"

Everyone wants someone to crawl back to;
everyone wants to forgive the rose for dying.

And this, from "Winged," an homage to the late Deborah Digges, a similar
large-hearted poet,

I recall how she skyhooked her keys
over her shoulder and into her jeep,
how she flipped her hair and smiled—
all earth, the woolen land that wears the rain—
professing the virus that lives
beyond the flesh in air.
The iridescence of buff and crown,
the terrestrial meadow singing.

And here, in a poem called "Nine-Dollar Bacon," she questions her own
self-worth after buying a rasher of bacon from a local co-op, concluding,

The vacuous cruelties are going to keep coming.
You're going to see something bad happen
to a child before the close of day. One of us
will get inoperable cancer, and it's enough to think
the rest of us would hold ice chips to the lips,
or at least think about it.

But for now—while the temperature is tolerable
while the bunnies and deer caper
freely among the madrona trees,
let us sing our drunken songs into the Pacific.
Let us cook up an indecent amount
of nine-dollar bacon before we head off
to wag our great, new fears at the bluffs.

Here then, a vital voice for our time, speaking in a way we can readily re-
ceive and remember, her voice both fragile and steely, Whitmanic but never
depressive. She praises and seeks, prays and exults. One of her strengths,
beyond that constant signature seeing, springs from her childhood aware-
ness of rural life now juxtaposed with her equally clear-eyed observations of
life in the city. She describes herself as a cosmic train moving

through the city as if in witness protection
from the country—the country a crime
we only commit when we forget who we are
in the dust soundtrack of the train-wheel's roar.

Laura Minor sings to us in sickness and in health, her poems like some wedding vow to us all in these precarious times. Her goal is clear:

I want to remember us as bodies
exhaling the odes of somewhere else,
fumbling for riotous liberty as unnamed slayers,
grass angels exercising their pastoral stupidity,
rising with empty cups to abandon the hour,
fall off the page. No matter what we do,
this revolving ball of dirt will turn
like a tea bag around a spoon.

And here, from her beginning poem, "Isolation Prayer," like a timeless invocation:

If the whole world kept still,
the prayer would rain humility,
laughing children,
the ear bones of Keats
into a bouquet to give you
the hand of God. We are lost
to the cosmos, but I tell you:

in the hour of nobody,
in the passport of loneliness,
and in the polar knife-edge of loss,
the body bends and the heart swings back
an axe of sighs.

Welcome, Laura Minor, to this broken fractal of a world that sternly measures us and still somehow offers chances for growth and self-awareness. Your poems are strong and vibrant and necessary. I already return to these poems for sustenance, and await with true anticipation the poems you are working on right now.

—John Hodgen
final judge, John Ciardi Prize for Poetry

Isolation Prayer

So that you can breathe,
the prayer is loose at the top of the world.
If the whole world kept still,
the prayer would rain humility,
laughing children,
the ear bones of Keats
into a bouquet to give you
the hand of your own god. We are lost
to the cosmos, but I tell you:

in the hour of nobody,
in the passport of loneliness,
and in the polar knife-edge of loss,
the body bends and the heart swings back
an axe of sighs.
Feed the dog
what she wants. Give the grieving streets
coins and their sisters.

Primal

Born in a river, O motherboard,
map of my circuitry—you made a star,
gave her a whole chocolate cake
for her sullenness held up like a tree fort
shot through and illuminated with fireflies—
how graceful their death-drops, which only birds
        and children could ever see.

But when those birds crooned together,
they shook the stores of our suffering—
tiny fists orchestrated the shadows,
        and the grass dressed up as fire.

The Ricketiest Song in the World

We're down to bare wood and fiberboard,
air washed and tung oiled and still,
        the borer bees are coming
      to destroy the only mechanism that holds
us together. Most nights, I wake up wet
      and we're under the Brooklyn Bridge
within the stacked music of apartments.

We were just two lonely dollar bills
shoved between tits at the last minute.
My black boots turn, whir with a friary rub
      under the sad paper of your absence.

I am exhumed, tired of grit,
drunk on predators, watching lightning
      cook the weeds around my feet.
I am ready to dive into bricks
looking for you. An affair is plastic, red nosed.
I want the muse that will drive me into the ground,
      blazing up the wet dirt of my own grave.

I plan to ambush you, to axe your ant farm,
and fresh from the bath, your fingers are pinched
      dumplings I want to burn against my breastplate

—yes, to take you, stick a knotted rag in your mouth,
      light the fucker, and watch you glow.

I have enough moisturizer to keep me in New York;
I have my workout and my pink hate—

but I'm tired of the smell of trash and the sight
of scarves lightly whipping the air with mockery,

the decayed tone of the man busking on the subway:
        guitar backpack, studded strap,
in-ear mic, and a bejeweled black hat,
        makes me want to pull out the pins
that hold this city together and catch you
in the bucket scoop of my arms.
        I am a cavernous, traveling siren
screaming slow jams, and yet, I'm not done
feeding the south with ballads
        that butter the sad mouths of strangers.

Exiled in Palatka

Trapped in a wraith of a town,
I need to exhale the prayer
of a roadside traveler
clasping the oyster moon
now graduating from its estuary.

This stretch of local tomatoes
weighing down the fences near Interlachen—
watching the kids sit barelegged
on roadside crates, legs dangling
like a donkey's tail, no address
except the buggy real estate of corn stalks,
the spell of their names in the fallen pecans.

What I crave is a nod to the dust that settles in layers
upon a picture frame the rag can't reach.
It takes going somewhere else
to find out what you've been missing
in a couple of onions hanging in old pantyhose
or strawberries banned for their shade of red.

How many times do I have to play Orpheus to myself
and fail? How many country songs do I have to become?

The best thing Ovid ever said about exile and loss,
        hungry from looking back, was

Volo tecum nullo modo possum.
I want to be with you
        any way I can.

So says the poet,
even in his hatred for Augustus,

even from his faraway Black Sea.

Aubade

With morning, and you
still in your pajama bottoms,
where night ends its dog-nose chill,
night with the prizefighter look,
night with eyes like a safe
that will never be unlocked,
night with teeth like the light
      backing into our knees.

Night with hands, needles, violins,
a mouth of wet sand—and dawn,
      like you, sliding on a white t-shirt.

You've Got the Whole House Fighting

There, sleeping inside the dog
is the patience of the unfolding sky.

Ask her now, how to rise
and dictate the stars

(and always,
I am the stars untied).

I found a cat in the alley outside the funeral home.
I also found a half-dead palm tree, exhausted,

having long stood witness to death.
Let's go home! Cold water for everyone!

Whitman for everyone! Everyone must grow
and fatten happily with meaning and affection

because tomorrow we will be crying
for mercy and justice. Tomorrow,

we will greet the day scraping.
The cat looked up at me,

Go to them with anything you've got.
Go to them with claws and teeth.

The half-dead palm sighed.

Real Town & Country

Once, a woman's musk on the train
conjured the pinch of my seaside youth
—briny, consistent in its waterlogged blessing. I waited out
my contract of subtropical longing, now here,
manifested in these splayed, commuters' bodies
peppered with wage and heat, lapping each other daily.

I bend down and boost you up, future self, older woman,
hold you up to the light—look at you—
you are so difficult to make out.

A bump on the underground tracks sends me from city
to arcadia, and again, I drink in the sun with you
from a ceramic limoncello decanter: here, all my summers
erect themselves like corpse flowers, rot away
in the cup of my green hands opened like a parted mouth.

In memory, brother is still triumphant on the deck,
holding up a dead eel framed by wood, water, and sky
where we briefly lived between the elements in an A-frame,
a spidery house standing, exaggerated in its puddle.

And there we are, still carving our names
in the air with cowfish, throwing them back
to the tusk of another day between worlds.

I am forever back and forth on a cosmic train
where I move through the city
as if in witness protection from the country—
the country a crime we only commit
when we forget who we are
in the dust soundtrack of the train wheel's roar.

Fall Invitation

I want to break my yolk,
ooze in public spaces,

caught in honey while the wheels of old dogs
slog through the dry bread of each day

toward paper children and poems. One day,
you will come in the night—

set my old desk on fire.

No—love me like you love your hands.
Come in from the cold,

leave the mouth of the river,
loosen, become the shipworm.

I'm ready to retract myself from the plank's ledge,
hole up in baskets of chips and bottled tea,

picnic the void and confess
to the matching blankets of your eyes.

Prayer for the Water to Hold Us

You never know your family
           until you're stuffed on a boat together;

we laugh with the same teeth and mouth, sail
           with the same sporting anger, losing

our land legs one ripple at a time, silent
           and dumb as the future knocking.

This is the magnificent story
           of ruining things, weeping bottles,

flying tuna-fish sandwiches.
           This is the broad expansion

of panic between waves, ears skimming
           the underwater saints between the walls—

a family sinks, a family rises—
           each heart undoing its particular gospel.

For Every Jesus, a Woman

Walking in the city, I stopped next to an older woman
looking into a grocer's shopwindow, and we both looked

for some kind of meaning, something beyond ourselves
found hanging in the caramel scroll of glazed duck bodies,

the most messianic corpses I'd ever seen. Her tired sneakers
pushed her ankle skin into puddles, her body, a dried ginger

root bent over a cane, her spine, curved under her sweater
like a conch shell. But the ball of her cheek

was definitely the back of a spoon gowning us both
in the pilfered city lights—blessings the size of dimes!

We hesitated to turn away from each other, mesmerized
by the fatty purses of animals, content in our shared humanity,

for now,
to have survived the mob's pyre.

Drinking to Excess After Much
Has Gone Wrong

When I see a lemon tree in bloom,
each golden orb plucking the lamplight
from the trees, it reminds me
     of vodka on ice, and how odd
that I never thought of lemonade,
its milk-droop swirl opposite the sweat.
Instead, I see gutted rinds curled like stretching dancers
     across the starburst of a cutting board.

Lemons strip you naked of the fat and lies,
     down to the slow mend of thigh and femur.
Lemons can end your grief's tin spinner

in one determined squeeze. I think of the backup
bottle of pre-squeezed juice slouching in the refrigerator door,
how I survived some of the bad days only when they were met
with a few sharp slaps of lemony reset.

It's best to mature and finish the job of ripening
instead of flashing through life
     like a cheap jewelry sale.

Until then, I wait and give in,
wrestle the dog with her pill,
always on the 20th, steady as checking
     the thermostat—or that first moment
you turn off the lights when leaving a room
to save money, or check the knobs on the stove
     so the place doesn't burn down—

Ode Calling Out John Hughes, Director

John Hughes—you've really screwed us,
I'm realizing now, driving back into Florida,
thinking about each of my exes' faces
as they spill into the scrub pines,
a watermelon truck bubbling past
a Winnebago. And always—*PEANUTS*—
written in chest-high script,
subtle pleasures pointing toward
one more hurricane-laced winter.
I am too weary for the banter your films impart.

What if the last scene in *Some Kind of Wonderful* ended
with the drummer choosing decadence and solos
over the noise of true love? What if
the studio suits allowed for the original ending
to *Pretty in Pink*, and she didn't choose the fantasy,
but instead, the poor oddball, and they bloomed
into a shabby bouquet of pink taffeta and bolero badness?

Or—what if no one chooses to couple, onscreen or off,
as you've shown us? What if people can be as you portray them:
a landscape of smug sunglasses, a cigarette resting on a lip,
those pulp-romance scenes that never exist
in my North Floridian montage of backroad orange stands
and their fading, sunny monologues, the cliché
of railroad tracks where we met to forage magic 'shrooms
against the odds of tomatoes, eyes of leaves
hearts of moss—what were we thinking
in our country hubris?

Pulling into the gas station, I dizzy myself
in the stain of winter, trying to believe
in the gut's pustuled highway; I refuse loyalty
in the sad eyes of dogs, now staring at me,
guarding a truck bed's crude carcass.

Can we sing for the buck stiffening in the chill?

I'm driving through my home state to no one,
no one waiting for me in a landscape of polluted fish.
I'm still looking for the fabled hallucinogen
in a farmer's fenced pen, my face bleached
by my lighter, undeterred
by the snorting bull beyond.

But John, I admit we also paw at your hope
in the face of our collective poverty;
my mind wants to be somewhere better
than this gas station parking lot in Starke, FL—
because the earth still does really have everything.

In the future, I know exactly what's waiting for me:
the same sweaty pulse of liquor, always the oysters,
and the bar's seasonal songwriter for the seafood circuit.

And what if one of your outsider heroes
with the cliffhanger jawline took me into the woods
and left me there to make me even more animal,
power-boundless, able to transcend my human form,
because animals don't judge each other
on the limits of desire and loins—

Florida knows me better than you do John,
knows that I'll always choose pleasure
over anything sustained by the courageously romantic.

So, I choose excess, infinite acts of whatever I can.
Give me the sky's distress of too many flowers,
sunny sexters, barroom sirens,
the pre-prelapsarian purity of orgasm;
my limits are an ocean. Give me Florida
as tipsy Roman gladiators stand
at the rim of fall, dancing,
spilling their wine onto someone's genitals.

Lungfish

I am a lungfish walking for the first time.
Here is the surf, the beach, and my feet

forming steps. And she is a holy psalm
of freckles along a spine, seducing me

out of the water with glass-blown eyes.
Her mouth opens like a half-eaten gate

and there is a small laugh hidden in that palace—
the death scene of her chin against red lipstick.

I fall into her hair, a harbor of stars
curling ocean stones into silt—Vertigo

wrapped in barrettes. Looking into her eyes,
two muted pigeons on black branches,

fugitives against the watery landscape,
shadows luring the tide from my lungs,

smoothing my gills into hips,
pulling out the white tide of one life,

breaking open the bubbled heart of another.

Unburden

My father dropped a scalpel on my weak spot
one summer afternoon, sun ambered through gravel
like sap; he told me to sit down in the living room.
      He told me
I couldn't call him *Dad*.

I wasn't to call him by his name either.
He said he didn't know what
      I was to call him.
He sloppily tried to avoid my eyes,
      and I went thick with familial pain—
a twin princess canopy with purple satin sheets—
      where I stayed. I cut his head

from the family pictures, placed them outside my door.
One night, I punched through a painting of a famous clown
he'd given me, tossed its frame out the window
      to mangle the midnight green in a twist of violet and plastic.

You have to put something
      of your own into the fight.

Later, staying with a friend nearer to the water,
my newly single mom sent *Charlie* perfume
with a forged note from my father. The rooms
changed again. My eyes became soup bowls.

Years grafted our tension to bad couches,
      as many as a decade would allow,
and we sagged low with the weight.

      But now, I often choose forgiveness,
and I can't explain it other than to say,
      I do not want to suffer through
each carpet pill of my life
      carrying old landmines on my shoe.

And it makes the living better,
a simple yes—
for a father who drinks his jaw full
before putting one foot in a shoe.

Our past will always be red-faced, puffing
outside the door, but I choose that girl

living near the ocean, her ponytail
flogging the air with slaughter
in the sweet church of separation,

the air a wonder as perfect
as the most finely tuned back-dive

into the perfumed letter of night.

Because We Will Not Always Be

When your eyes are too old to read,
and books cease to swoop and attack
(like the child free from the stoop
leaping into crowds of pigeons),
think of me; nature,
cruel in its blazing craft,
      will turn my arms to dirt.

I will turn myself into rain.
I will stand on the edge
and shake out the trees for you.
I will open a small sea for you,
and put my ear to the highest window
      to see if it compares to you.

Edward Leedskalnin, 1887-1951,
Raised the Coral Castle

His only freckled courtship, soapy sculptures—
lost purity whips men to the tussled math of derangement,
to the crumbled walls of devotion unraveled.

He set his stone garden in the night like a coral,
a womb in itself, breathing in the distance of stars
from his hands' furious occupation. To magnetize us,
the energy grid beneath our feet.

The Feast of Love Table, the world's largest valentine,
just gray vapors of oolite limestone.

Ghosted by the children who haunted the walls for a look,
alone in the balmy midnight music of owls,
drunk down by *The Moon Fountain*,
crossed like the North Star—

he seized a scoop of madness in the world,
a phenomenon of decades in the detritus of longing,
electrified monuments erected to the ideal of women
and not the women themselves.

Amassed out of the moors of the mind, permanent homes
for the offering—
no one gossips about corals,
animals of destruction able to materialize
in neon churches and stagger the stride of the stars—

love is not an earthen monster.

To Be Alone Is a Gift

Those who I never wanted have been eating my light,
unfolding like new lawyers fresh from school—

     still, the blue sky has always been the online stuff of birds.

Do not curb this Saturday lament. A waterfall moves
between the rocks of women, wishes
soon expired, surrounding each of us. When I say:

take me to the work

of living life alone, and let me clean
all the baseboards low to remember,
     to assume the position of slowly eclipsed, falling
     forward in years, people and their oval faces,
     the creamy footprints of distant beaches—

this is my King and my Kung Fu.

Open Window on State St.

I think of the Russian woman who stayed in my loft,
sleeping naked on the fire escape with a blur of a man
who'd wandered into the party. She left a star
            on my inner left ankle with a needle
and a small pot of ink. I can still see her shrugging
from the window of that place, where we got up games
of Wiffle ball, led by our roommate,
            a maudlin dilettante studying law.

Extraordinary women unpack themselves
like dirt around water. She was one woman,
and not a vision or a friend to me for more than a day.
But she reminded me of Ama,
whose name is an Italian conjugation for love,
a dear one who wears her burden with the weight
of St. Augustine's confessions—

and at night her eyes are up-turned umbrellas in wind.

Ama lives on the Florida coast and there is a wildness
inside of her that slips out and eats the turquoise algae
pickling the tide. She looks into the infinite face
of the water with more muscles than winged Samothrace,
still composing her short story,
which she believes will be famous for its silver sands.

It's in her name to transition
past the collapsed attic of her years,
to slink away from being a walking vagina to men,
or a lightning bolt, or whatever else the world
tells a woman she must be,
unaware of what still counts as possibility.

Our influencers say with no sense of their irony:
You have to be your own cheerleader.
And that's the worst part: to jump in one place,
breaking down the same patch of dirt
      like a spot you can't get out.

But there was that Russian woman
who visited me on State St., how she climbed
onto that fire escape, straddling it, tanned legs
hanging one on and one off,
a lampshade gathering all the light,
      then diffusing it to the sidewalk below.

In the Lilacs

Do not come crawling like a whelp
To my flowerbed. Come
In a tall flame on the living
Window-petaled pane of day.
Come to my bed in rivets and rags
And mud-soiled moans.
We will become fan blades of sex, muscle, and bone.
We will turn lilacs shameless to the night
And feed on myth where
I will hear your voice as low, lavender music
Roaring in the ardent green.

I Don't Camp Well

You can't reason with deer anymore than the sunlight.
Unafraid of me, they can't be rushed away from their grazing,
here with me watching behind the screen door of this cabin—

they make me want children
which makes me hate their faces,
their near-human eyes making me want
more from the potential of a home.

Even now, as the deer stand close enough
to kiss the jasmine bushes, the adults together,
and their fawn, knock-kneed in the fuzz of morning—

I want to stay inside the tent of my mind,
paint my nails black and make fun
of my friends who gleefully kayak—
stupid, noble crayons of the sea.

꒕ ꒕ ꒕

Once, when a boyfriend wanted to look
for the famed wild horses of Cumberland Island,
I wanted a different natural magic
away from the uniform confusion of coupling.

I left him standing in that field and found myself
caught between the warning grunt of a mama boar
and thirteen wild horses. I caught a milky yearling
with spots out of the right corner of my eye.
Coupling and terror are just two trees
in the same shallow water, roots commingled
with the sea level's dooming groan, and me,
the lone, winsome variable of nature.

With Guitar in Hand

On the slow descent, down the last hill home,
I could say to myself: *It's not too late.*
But my neighbor pops over unannounced
with a dwindling beer, false astonishment—

her boy is *having sex.* And somewhere between
I haven't done meth since 2007
and *I hate my dog,* she says

if you haven't had a kid by now,
eyes plated with booze, *might as well not.*

She begs me to play her a song,
one she knows from before babies,
like Bon Jovi. I want her to go back
down the hill to her new husband
who can't fall asleep without her.
They've been fighting on my phone
about the third dog. He accused her
of wanting to castrate his only pit bull.
But she wants to do what is best,
wants to stay here under the mushroom cap
of my intended badlands. I convince her
she needs to go home, and she makes a somber,
four-point turn in her vehicle that ambles
like an old black bear back into the smokestack woods.

I imagine her idly walking up to her front door,
dogs around her like fluttering, dirty muses.

A Fairly Serious Relationship

I met him because I wanted to meet him
and there he was, on tour with my friends—
his brand seeded in the ease
     of flaxen self-hatred—
averting the smiling eyes of *woman writer*.

During his show, I materialized, slipping through
that punk club's cocksure pillars with a twelve-pack.
     But he was blanketed fresh afterbirth, a fresh straw
sleeping on top of my shoes, in my closet, so afraid
of my hunger like all the others—
loud signs ripped from the gates of youthful direction.
     There is one other way to say this:
when I think of what latticed illusion
fills my bedroom window now,
     my core swells with the trapeze
of that summery stumble.
     Budding plants, romance as hologram,
scarecrows walking our self-loathing dreams:
are we really sorry
     for deconstructing the ones we want,
for building them up too high just to vilify them,
blossoming sculptures of antiquity slowly eroding,
     desperate as public pamphlets in the street?
We won't always survive each other—but there is kinship
in words, in the impoverished sanctuary of a closet floor,
desire negotiated—scooped brilliance
     on which to rest your woozy vim.

Recidivism

Your bullpen jumpsuit was bright orange
    on the morning I told the judge you were a good man.

Months later, the terrible applause of pool balls
    rolled through me as I walked home

and the heft of summer anchored me
    from flinging myself into trees.

    The women on the street came in shapes
like the smooth bodies of guitars.

Everyone wants someone to crawl back to;
    everyone wants to forgive the rose for dying.

    You used to make everyone jealous of my laughter,
        turned every moment vignette, borderless and fading.

What Was Here, If Not Angels

I don't want to name you, *Greg*.
          Quotidian *Greg*, you are not here
in this conference hotel room where I imagine
you as my first fallen snow,
the class letting out early so the girl from the panhandle
          could see it fly from the sky's mush.
I had my own rebound with forgiveness, that slinky toy.
          It sprang down the stairs of this decade
into the slop bucket of a fight in the park
where we would do our best to panic and tear down
the thing just for it to bobble back up
          in the womanly curves of Jumbo's Clown Room
          and Echo Lake full of lotus blossoms—
I don't want to walk by those ducks mating again
as the male drowns her in an act of courtship.

                    ᵛᵛᵛ

I'm nervously idling here in LA,
but now, as a professional.
All I want is a laying on of hands
as I pass the mountain we once hiked
          in hopes of seeing our little settlement reflected
          in the cosmos, or rather, the promise of it.
But all the glass of that world needs a good wiping.
          Here, writing in this downtown hotel,
my colleague trolls the well for distraction and sport,
the failures drift down in lazy truffles, every one unique,
every one a challenge to the inherent labor
in my own *Three Billy Goats Gruff*—
          my favorite childhood story—
ending in a tough goat fatally butting
          life's evilness into the river.

Even the ancient adorations from my youth, I see them again
        in this familiar, neon signage off Sepulveda Blvd.,
in the red shine of a Silver Lake barstool,
on the strip where jumpsuited Scientology grunts
        rake away their stories in the prehistoric exchange
of ground and foot. I can forget
our desperate getaway to Big Sur, but not the coastline,
        its rocky intercourse stringing the tourist cabins together
like links in a prisoner's waist chain;
                        our strange contract of hope on display
like the elephant seals barking and bumping,
        their slicked chests—ready to slip away.

❧ ❧ ❧

I guess I just wanted to see snow falling from the sky.
I wanted to be dismissed as just another woman
in the montage who needed a moment to revise
her failed expectations across a continent.

And you, reader, with whom I am sharing
this story of all fallacious angels—
doesn't it always go back to forgiveness and resistance,
        craving and aversion, the languorous pulse
of Jumbo's Clown Room as your friend gets a lap dance,

the Los Angeles air thick with Tiki-Ti smoke, and a drink,
the blue sugar of a dream fragrant with violent duck sex
and the blinding flash of lotus blossoms?

Winged

for, and after, Deborah Digges

When she bloomed like vervain,
did the fever bird tire and fly
backward over her right shoulder?
When she rode *the light's poor spine*
to earth, to touch down in gutters,
in the rainbowed urine of suicides,
the content of her veins
made all the flowers brighter.

From that place, she stared at ruin,
and ruin stared back. The pitch of wall
gave way to a single starling's flight,
as she saw the thinning heads of buildings,
every nail, change the address of her mind.

Greeting her in the parking lot once,
I recall how she skyhooked her keys
over her shoulder and into her jeep,
how she flipped her hair and smiled—
all terra, the woolen land that wears the rain—

professing the virus that lives
beyond the flesh in air.
The iridescence of buff and crown,
the terrestrial meadow singing.

Leaving Baby Island

Amen, Amen, Amen. O womb, womb, womb, cylindrical womb, red womb,
white womb, fleshy womb, bleeding womb . . . O demoniacal one!
–from a tenth century European prayer to cure hysteria

I tell her, I want to move.
I want to finish something I started, or begin something
I've neglected. We talk
the way we're supposed to when someone has to leave,
            endeared, tenuous—yes, her hair—
rosé washing over bolts of Texas plains,
splintered like the pastel halves of chopped firewood—

            my girlfriend doesn't want me to leave New York,

to pick up my distractions like disassembled track lighting
and set them on the nightstand near our temples.
            She throws her hair into my face.

I imagine watching this neighborhood's tank advance
of double strollers get sucked into a dust cloud
from my window's aperture—
            she wants me to unpack my case, stay, and build a life
            the way she makes product replicas for films.
I talk about identifying
            as a point of light on a sphere
            and how the stuffed dog I gave her
really does look like her dog—
the point is that I saw my mother eat only spaghetti
with butter and garlic salt for a year, the only year
            she would ever be a single, adult woman—
the charming lie of ideal parenthood—
            trauma nestled in a noodle coma.

Yes, to those of us who choose our weightlessness,
            who step off the island and change the zip code—

the shadow gods who birth light,
            gifting ourselves back to the world.

The Lost Body a Music Makes

for Jeff Buckley

I still look for him digging in his pockets,
change for the falafel cart. Even the scientists
      in Antarctica I read about,
the ones who drank themselves into the madness of ice,
into time's explosive quicksand, stopped and looked north,
      offered up their distant kindling as his foothold.

If I scream the wine off my own throat's slide, his decrescendo
will still not climb down from death's infant suck.
      His croon still tows the Mississippi
through my glittering buckle of blood. His chords still tremble
through the silken woodland of my mother's ironed hair,
      each note haloed—*Hallelujah*

      to the impossibility of all breath, *Hallelujah*
revisited late in the drowning man's dirge—
to the impossibility of more with a faraway brunette
to the impossibility of a living father's fugal harmony,

Hallelujah to all who still breathe, everyone
      made up of a stadium of bones, machinery, and time—
the lost body a music makes.

The Murder Hole, Brooklyn, NY, 2011

In that apartment, where summer paced out its loss,
even the paint couldn't last. I binge-watched
my life in a televised haze, clicked past
       my apocalyptic storefront, the door,
       a purgatory facing an expressway.

Standing in the shower, I beat its corners into songs,
as one man after another
       turned me into an ampersand—

that year, I finally made my list of names.
To the laurel of the girl I was:
to the graveyard spirits of Dear You's,
       the back-and-forth of the pas de deux,
never seeing myself, just a slash of lipstick
for fieldwork, fingering the fake pearls
       spilling over my clavicle,
       a wave with a foaming crest,

with a face that settled a room
like a machine gun solves an argument.

Never wanting the party to end,
       I peeled and sectioned myself like a tangerine,
ran tripping down the stairs of anyone
       to kiss them through a screen.

Like the figures in Larkin's "Arundel Tomb,"
I make myself a historical event, never finished.
And in my stone wimple, I ask myself who cares
if he cheated on her, if she cheated on him—
       we're all just voltage and hands on the big slab.

Aqua Queen

for Esther Williams

What did she see underwater when she emerged
from the oversized clamshell, was she
glad? Was she, like us, hoping
the water would heal us whole? When
she poured herself from the bubbling pinhead
of a Hollywood geyser into the depths
of those soundstage pools like someone holding
warm syrup high over a plate—
       she was willing to swim through it all, become the tilde,
the accent slithering around life's underwater pole,
her most fantasy-soaked moments, a dream
that would never dare look away. And why should it?

No one
wants to look away

from the athletic prowess of a flower in a storm, water
as it leaves your face, one more way
for us to survive, to watch each other survive
something harder than water—
       that ebullient resistance
             that always gives way.

Elegy for Marina without the War and Famine

Job in a skirt
—Joseph Brodsky on Marina Tsvetaeva

I want to know, Marina, what is left
after this lonely, leggy pout
has put years on us—

Marina, your grief-bangled eyes
pull me into your rooms, shake me, ask me
about the swaying eyelets of your shoes,

ask me if I want some of the same:
She'll never survive
the cruelty of the age.

You're at the bedside table
scattering light again. Your body's
on the sill, unlaced, white and green

the ocean fills and comes. Take me
to you—we're indifferent and weary
of luxury—sunny checkbooks and potato stew.

Home State

In Florida, it's always noon and everything is full of honey
—Jack Gilbert

Mother, forgive me the days I sang alone.
Remember me as the child learning to write
in a sand-colored room wrought
with the Gulf's ringing, and you
in that faded navy one-piece, marbled
like a Florida moon that drags its chunk
up the rise of the coasts nightly,
speaking its aberrant gospel—Florida,

I was born in the hands of fronds, and for now,
nothing can keep me from your hothouse fissure,
you dune of delight, you querulous flash
upending the sinkhole's lunar allure.

Flowers as Mind Control

I want the good Parmesan,
the thinly shaved stuff they keep in the cheese cooler that stands
alone. This morning, I wanted to kill myself.
But I can't get to New York for a last slice,
      so this Parmesan will have to do.

I look at Myrtle,
      my dog that will not go
when it's been storming,
        even if it's been days.
I thought, *You saved me once.*
      I should get the good cheese,
          for you, who are weirdly afraid.

I could feel the silence that belongs to everyone
as I pulled into my very last parking spot.
      I'd been crying for a time, and the rain
made the town bloat like a fresh bun.
      And then, the cute man
I saw the other night at the bar walked toward my car—

              I will say the flowers here in Tallahassee
              are really something. I use them as
        nostalgic symbols for when my brain and my heart

were calm, when I used to watch my brother
      fall asleep on a blanket my mother made
from velvety scraps, and it was always
in front of a sliding glass door while it rained—

if the cute man walks into the store, now,
just a passing pair of downcast frames,
I'll go home, do all the things I have to do,
      and make sense of this phantom moment tomorrow,

but he passed the store and kept walking—

it's funny how we haggle away our most precious gifts
for stories of romance fumbled down like a game of *Telephone*.

I bought a tomato and drove home.

I thought about my cousin who overdosed
        in a seaside motel—
how awful we are when our cards are pressed
to the level of dread. The last time I felt like this,
I was buried in the specifics of a bagel I shared with a friend,
and he told me that I really needed to get laid.

        At this point, you're thinking
        that I have a problem with food.
        But I don't. And this age
        is troubling enough for a person to strap
        an explosive vest to their body
        and pull the ripcord on everyone's misery—

I'm not going to kill myself.
        I'm certain that by tomorrow,
I will be a great person. I'm someone, a rare flower.
        I have pictures to prove it.

New Girl at the Seed Factory

Then you, clutching a bag of Drum tobacco,
wishing the wanton slush under your boots would turn white

again. And me, assigned to shipping
five people back, wondering what you wear around the house.

The indifferent guy with the new timecards says,
Three days sick, one minute in late,
        one minute out early, and you get docked—

all these seeds, and nothing grows.

He tells us more Vietnamese workers are coming:
      We're gettin' a shitload of 'em in today,
like a pallet of pepper pods no one wants to unload before break.

And earlier, Larry with a knit cap full of sin followed you inside,
      asking for a ride to Philly after work.

You're always humming over the conveyor belt
and on the loading dock at lunch where you roll
      three cigarettes in a row, eat raw garlic,
        wary of the *DANGER—HIGH VOLTAGE* sign.

      I broke the tape gun once so you would have to talk to me.

For now, I hear you packaging the expense of days till summer.
      I see the meteor resting on the wedge cradling your kidneys,

for now—hurl us like stones across the belt
      where the label-maker prints maps on our bodies,
where we bust through this line on the way to the parking lot,
      rip the safety gloves from our hands,
bare our greasy chests—
      sweaty buds saluting the city sun.

Pocket Change

Having spent the night
with the random 2x4 propped
at the ready against the chipped, red door—

and with her fears as they ripple
through the domestic bedlam of their planets—
        she wants to transform and plunge down from herself.
She thinks of a rosy-cheeked teen eagle hunter
high on a mountain who she once saw on the internet,
and that bird of prey springing from the embroidered perch of her arm
down into a rodent-littered ravine where peonies grow.

The winter coat on the chair has pockets full of old, loose pills:
        one for youth, one for disease, and one for recreation.

All the rooms!
        The dulcimer, restrung on its stand to the far wall,
its curvature bronzed by the sunlight,
where the marble bust of a woman turns away
from the breath tipping out of the delphiniums,
        and her favorite books leaning into each other
are not enough to stop the nights when gravitational waves
        swallow even the idea of light.
Or   how loud the refrigerator is?
Or   Sylvia Plath, dead 55 years,
        she read earlier in the day.
And coins that end up buried in the dirt,
        having once meant something to a kid,
now lie flatly in the bottom of a heavy purse.

Reunion

The broken-down dream recovered! She wasn't
just a gilded egg, something left to be found,
surviving in the bush until I came along.

I leave her alone—
O my true dream, she's a weak thing
that doesn't need some browning tea rose
pinned to her lapel for the little reunion,
rescued rather than excavated,
where instead of some piteous debt, she ignores
her thickened fingertips pushing a street-corn cart
      uphill in the colonized desert,
      clouds of pork skins,
postured and buff, ballooning from all sides—

      she dies and becomes anything to bring me back
to the beach, the trees, where I'm not stuck
in a lead barrel, weeping in a jar, a sigh dipped out
      the size of a lion's ear—

this is when I live and succumb to the ocean's fuel,
      the money is more than we all counted on,
and whatever this thorny blanket of pink hydrangea,
the dues of my veteran womanhood—that
      is what I am sleeping on tonight.

For Want of You

after Rites of Spring, in memoriam of Travis

They patted your ashes into the tree pit's loam
    under the cultural center's greatest oak.

Once, you took your glasses off before bed ...
    the room, the room in the world

was as pained and delicate as anything I'd seen before—
    every new day slatted you like blinds.

Now, you—my common hero,
    roots coiled in clay and sprig.

After the funeral, I revisited a dusky drag of sky
    and you saying—
        you never know love until you ride bikes together.

Once, you were hesitant about brushing my hair,
    as if my hair itself could hurt you

[I want you back until we can discuss this over coffee].

    Here is my great lie:
We had a real Ginsbergian hope then.

Like butterflies loosed from their gauzy ward,
    now, only the wind gladdens our tires—

I choose your laugh, hands cupped around your mouth,
    body rocking, back and forth,

back and forth—
on the ride home, I pressed into the wheel,
    listening, still stunned at how they said punk rock started.

Something had to be done, but no one knew what to do,
    or how to change it all, and I kept pressing,

leaning into the steering wheel, pressing
    into my black dress with the white dots,
        the luminous scholarship of the stars.

Nine-Dollar Bacon

Who is doing the work here?
That we should be so lucky
to escape our respective poverties,
our cheating spouses or the collective foot
we elect for our necks, even when we are
poets in America—is there anything
more decadent? Maybe Florida, maybe
this rasher of nine-dollar bacon
I just bought at the local co-op.

I see my friends talking outside on the porch
as I'm frying it up. One has escaped
his brutal youth, kept outside like a dog
to drink from the hose. And I want to feed him
bacon—thick-cut, hickory-smoked, nine-dollar bacon
that I imagine has been handled by women with plump fingers,
nipples the size of peaches,
eager and willing to feed the miserable world.

And another friend whose heart was thrown
like a newspaper against the side of her own house—

she deserves some bacon, enough to build
a palace of nine-dollar bacon for her
and her son to hide in, nibble on the walls,
speaking the language of the lonely family
kissing the salt from each other's wounds.

And myself—
what about me?

Am I worthy of my own nine-dollar bacon?
I've done my share of weird & selfish things,

and I've beaten myself up pretty good.
I've had enough small injustice

to admire the man stocking the shelves with bacon.
Give the aging writer nine-dollar bacon
because she can't remember love's fresh swirl.

The vacuous cruelties are going to keep coming.
You're going to see something bad happen
to a child before the close of day. One of us
will get inoperable cancer, and it's enough to think
the rest of us would hold ice chips to the lips,

or at least think about it. But for now—
while the temperature is tolerable,
while the bunnies and deer caper
freely among the madrona trees,
let us sing our drunken songs into the Pacific.
Let us cook up an indecent amount
of nine-dollar bacon before we head off
to wag our great, new fears at the bluffs.

In Fellini's *Nights of Cabiria*,
the Eponymous Female Lead Survives

I'm holding a napkin, ready to smite a cockroach
dashing across the floor. It wants nothing more
than to go forward, find some fuel and devour life.

I need a meteor to push through
this bloody cup of years,
        not a boil of stairs and doors—

it's either stay and make a life in Brooklyn
or go find a way in Costa Rica or another
fertile tract where expats get happier.

        It doesn't always have to be
leaves in the face, mud in the hair,
crying into the elbow of a cliff—

I'm saving myself from the heart's autumnal wreckage,
        just as Cabiria does at the end—
the air of decision is   swagger and sway,
        lean and kiss.

I will the wind to dust me off!
I will the tide below to wad its fists
and vanish as I amble back
to the plum blossoms of my people.
Semi-inflated with the dignity of survival & bound for home,
I gratefully punch through another midnight chill—

In Fractals of Matter on Earth
Where Heaven Is a Metaphor for Heaven

I want to live, to beat this lissome infection
that has scattered throughout my body
like children playing a game of hide 'n' seek
inside the glowing rooms of my organs for years.
Now, I am live aeration in the IV room,
lined up in a La-Z-Boy alongside other sick people
in a wondrously confused performance
for the world's infirm—I conjure you, poets,
into this facility, armed with the justice of magic,
and ask you to insulate our misery from the world.
Come close! And line this hyperbaric chamber
with the scratching of escape! Blow up all our veins,
branch our futures in bruise-art along the walls
of this oxygenated coffin—we are all *"Shephard,"*
misspelled on the nurse board. Echo the language
and choreograph with me a mechanized network
of spirochetes in lines that run off the page.
I call up your priestly muse! Erato rides again!
Marshals of Weirdness! Tear down the walls
of this bee-less mountain—believe in the truth
of resuscitation, the beautiful impermanence of mulch.
Even this terror-field of death has a few sunflowers!
Your words create a blood subway threaded
with the rise and fall of thermometers. This room,
once a drab procession of pleather baubles, is now
a thankful hootenanny of carcasses redeemed, a portly sigh
of exaltation—my vitals, my vitals, endless as footsteps—
I look to you in gratitude and wave my hooked arm like a wand!

Everything Beautifully Sideways

In the pub, thick with smoke
and various fake penguins,
we three friends tip out
the golden coattails of last call,
scurry a bottle to a nearby field
to lean between the thighs of two small hills,
and drink to our newness in want with words—
this is the moment we choose
wilderness instead of rooms.

We sit and talk away the coolness of soil
until no one mistakes this for anything else,
and we are just a tangle of luxury in the grass,
a triangle of bodies holding up the sky—

three newly introduced poetry students
and a bottle of good whiskey.
Chaos cannot shoulder us in this field.
And what you think of your friends
on the first night you really talk with them,
the first fun, will soon turn astringent
in the inclement weather of everyday
betrayals and secrets revealed, changing
into different people, flowers more horrid
than when in bloom, now disguised as topsoil.

But this grass doesn't know the future.
In this moment, one friend needs his wife,
and the other, his duende is buried
in some cavity where there lives
a fountain of youth that can never be young.

Tomorrow, someone is still going to need
the brightest green shirt of a year, a job,
someone who'll forgive our August

seaside whimper; soon, my friends,
we are going to destroy each other.
Someone will be rejected, left leaning
into the shell of their hands, someone
will break a window to get a little air—

I want to remember us as bodies
exhaling the odes of somewhere else,
fumbling for riotous liberty as unnamed slayers,
grass angels exercising their pastoral stupidity,
rising with empty cups to abandon the hour,
fall off the page. No matter what we do,
this revolving ball of dirt will turn
like a tea bag around a spoon.
And no worry; friends will always stay
with each other for the want of what is greater—
to that simplicity, I say *yes*,
if this can just be three friends in the grass
instead of what we've known,
ripped and piled high, pea tendrils
thrown in a bowl—

give me the terrestrial against the old,
the ancient text of air and other for another go.

Supplication by the Sea on Labor Day

The air dyeing Anastasia Island,
    the conch-shell pink I love.

The sand-sugared beachgoers leaning
into the mid-drop of their morning—I love.

Worshippers asking the maritime gods for one more
    handspun strawberry milkshake to light
the small mussels barnacled to a piece of driftwood, I love.

    And the so-named Right Whale
somewhere off the first coast with her calf

        [their trill that marries this day
        to the labor of any birth].

I watch their tentacle business reaching out to the ether of gulls
with their mustard-shot beaks lined up for hours, miles!
to screech in anticipation of fish. Is there anything
still more vulnerable
    than being barefoot in a temple,

no work, no worries
    but the labor of breathing?

Bildungsroman in Red

I call you to that torn, leather couch
sprouting opium balls on the cherries
of imaginary cigarettes. We glow
like twin redheads, whole countries leave
their daughters to careless cowboys
and here—
        I am tender as a mouth.

Like breaking a wine bottle off a rock
and pretending the shards are ocean glass—
        this cannot be neat.

Every hesitation in me is set to snag.

O cinematographer,
the great American wedding cookies
swim around our heads like an infant's mobile.
O astronomer, can you send the satellite footage
of me as your wanton drifter—

timorous, thin-skinned skater that spilled through
        and survived like a death spiral
                survives the drain's ledge?

On that couch, I become a red blouse
with a fishbone pattern peeking through, my boot heel
dug in the wine-stained edges, a smashed skyline
        burnished as any newborn.

Manifesto for the New World

For those who live in the twisted nightgown of madness
For the hungry that sate with what's left of the leaves
For those who have never seen the ocean—
    I am the ear of god's blue trumpet.

For women who fall down in the dark and lift with dawn
For children biting their lips in war's opened cage

For the soldier's temples crying at dusk—
    I am the antenna jutting out of Mercy's hardware.

For the devils that sing in the prisoners' ears
For the eyes of those dying in the sun—

I am your water, your bandaged healer, whose hair
    falls around you, whose hair
falls around you on the floor.

Someone, I tell you, in another time will remember us.

    —Sappho

I'm kissing you now—across
the gap of a thousand years.

    —Marina Tsvetaeva

Acknowledgments

I would like to thank the poets I've worked with over the years: Sean Singer, Erin Belieu, David Kirby, James Kimbrell, Barbara Hamby, Billy Collins, Ilya Kaminsky, Marie Howe, Joan Larkin, Andres Rojas, Jennifer Knox, Jillian Weise, Tiffany Melanson, Suzanne Gardinier, Gerald Stern, Steve Lambert, Ed Pavlić, Robert Lopez, Andrew Epstein, Chris Jensen, Enid Shomer, Juan Carlos Galeano, Ben Furnish, Cynthia Beard, BkMk, and John Hodgen for their all-encompassing wisdom and guidance over the years that I have come and gone from poetry. I would like to extend inspired thanks and rest in peace to former mentors and teachers: Thomas Lux, Deborah Digges, Steve Orlen, and Ntozake Shange. And to all my friends and family who read poems, then, now, and forever—you are the contents of my heart and gratitude.

Many thanks to the editors of the following publications:

"Frolicking in the Land of Slaughter," a poetry chapbook record read by the author at the *EAT POEMS!* Press Series, University of North Florida, featuring the following poems: "Home State," "Nine-Dollar Bacon," "The Ricketiest Song in the World," "Open Window on State St.," "Exiled in Palatka," "Aubade," "The Murder Hole, Brooklyn, NY, 2011," "Recidivism," and "Everything Beautifully Sideways." —Fall, 2018.

"Aubade," "Isolation Prayer": New Rivers Press Anthology, *Wild Gods: The Ecstatic in Contemporary Poetry and Lyric Prose*

"Real Town & Country": *Ploughshares* (forthcoming)

"The Murder Hole ...": *North American Review*

"In Fractals of Matter ..." and "Isolation Prayer": *The South Carolina Review*

"I Don't Camp Well": *The Missouri Review*

"Aubade," "Because We Will Not Always Be": *Quiddity International Literary Journal & Public-Radio Program*

"Pocket Change": *Powder Keg Magazine*

"Bildungsroman in Red": *Arc Poetry Magazine*, Canada

"Exiled in Palatka": *American Poetry Journal*

"Recidivism," "Open Window ...": *O:JA&L*

"Home State": *Fantastic Floridas* (Burrow Street Press)

"Nine-Dollar Bacon": *Berfrois*, UK

"Flowers as Mind Control": *Queen Mob's Teahouse*, UK

"With Guitar in Hand": *Hobart*

"Leaving Baby Island," "Manifesto": *Trivia: Voices of Feminism*

"Elegy for Marina ... ," "Reunion": *Sixers Review*

"Prayer for the Water to Hold Us": SpringGun Press

"Primal": *jmww: A Quarterly Journal of Writing*

"In the Lilacs": *Mantis*, inaugural issue, Stanford University

"Lungfish": *Sarah Lawrence Review*

"New Girl at the Seed Factory": *Apalachee Quarterly*

"Everything Beautifully Sideways": *Normal School*

Laura Minor was a finalist for the National Poetry Series and is the author of the audio-only chapbook *Frolicking in the Land of Slaughter* (EAT Poems, 2018). She won the I.L.A.'s Rita Dove Poetry Award (chosen by Marilyn Nelson), the Sassaman Graduate Creative Writing Award, and the Emerging Writers Spotlight Award (chosen by poet D.A. Powell). Her poetry is forthcoming or has most recently appeared in *Ploughshares, North American Review, The Missouri Review, The Normal School, South Carolina Review, Quiddity International Literary Journal, Arc Poetry Magazine, Hobart,* and the 2021 New Rivers Press anthology, *Wild Gods: The Ecstatic In Contemporary Poetry and Prose.* She was a Teachers College Fellow at Columbia University and was chosen by Denise Duhamel for a Sarah Lawrence Poetry Award.

BkMk Press is celebrating its fiftieth anniversary in 2021. After thirty-eight years at the University of MIssouri-Kansas City, BkMk is returning to being an independent press in 2021. BkMk Press is grateful for the support it has recently received from the following organizations and individuals:

Missouri Arts Council
Miller-Mellor Foundation
Neptune Foundation
Richard J. Stern Foundation for the Arts
Stanley H. Durwood Foundation
William T. Kemper Foundation

Anonymous
Dwight Arn
Beverly Burch
Jaimee Wriston Colbert
Maija Rhee Devine
Ben Furnish
Charles Egan
Alice Friman
Anna Jaffe
Whitney and Mariella Kerr
Carla Klausner
Lorraine M. López
Patricia Cleary Miller
Margot Patterson
Peppermint Creek Theatre Company
Elizabeth Goldring Piene
Alan Proctor
James Hugo Rifenbark
Roderick and Wyatt Townley